Euphrasy: from Medieval Latin *eufrasia,*
from Greek *euphrasia* gladness, from
euphrainien to make glad.

for Marie

Euphrasy

Michael Shann

Paekakariki Press

2012

This is number **104**
from an edition
of 250 copies.

© 2012 Michael Shann
www.michaelshann.com
Illustrations by Helen Porter

Set in
12pt Garamond
by
Speedspools, Edinburgh

Printed at the
Paekakariki Press, Walthamstow
paekakarikipress.com

ISBN 978-1-908133-04-5

Euphrasy

The Three of Us

'The size of your fingernail,' it says in the book.
Or the tip of one frond of all the lemon-fern
we've walked through in the hills above Glendalough.

You at six weeks, queasy at times and ready for a nap
on any dry patch of green. This time you've dropped off
with whorls of orange peel and an open book in your lap.
Sheen of your sleep, your eyelashes' filigree shadows recall
the young girl I never knew and the mother I've yet to meet.

I look down on the shimmering ellipse of the lake,
as small and blue as the lapis stone in the ring I gave you
that early winter in Kathmandu.

Duckboards rise and fall across the bog.
When you wake we'll follow their tapering trail
till we reach the vanishing point of our coupled lives.

'Its heart will already be formed,' the book says.
And beats imperceptibly, soundlessly, still tentatively,
like this pink-flowering heather in the late-summer sun.

Birthday

Each sweet year since we moved here
I've walked out on the eve of your birthday
when we'd settled you all in your beds,
and in the dark March garden I've gathered
the fallen camellia blooms, big as rosettes,
pink and frivolous as blown wonders,
when held up to the stars,
from the ocean's interstellar depths.

And if there weren't enough blooms
I've plucked more blossom straight from the tree
until the bucket was pink brimming and ready.
Then I've dribbled a new number across the grass,
letting the wet waxy petals slip through my fingers
like the days we've had no days to remember.

And when the number was large on the lawn
I've stepped back, knowing it wouldn't be seen
properly, in proportion, until soon after dawn
when you peeped between curtains
for proof of how old you suddenly were.

Ammonite

One hundred and fifty million years old,
I say, handing over the shell's
clear impression, my fossil find,
a small grey gift of limestone.

You look it over with infant hands,
run a finger over filigree ribs,
but the years mean less to you
than they do to me

and I've been putting off telling you
that childhood lasts forever until it's over,
but then suddenly it's over forever.

Annomite, you giggle, knowing it wrong.
Annomite, annomite, but it won't come.
Still time, I say. You are pretty young.

Quid

These things too transcend the generations.
An ice-cream van still diffuses 'Greensleeves'
through miles of wet Saturday afternoons.
Plinky, allegro notes remember lives
absorbed in their adult occupations
(Ercolano's startled cast of captives):
the father rocking his daughter to dreams;
the grandmother sweeping her yard of leaves.

The music stalls, then you hear it again,
not so loud, receding, lifting more heads
from their interests, streets away to the west.
And somewhere a child is running towards
this tune unaware of the ash-light rain.
He holds the warming coin tight in his fist.

Walthamstow Triptych

1 – Lullaby

Winter wind in the chimney
is an old, companionable sound,
as old as the house,
cooing softly through the night
like a solitary owl,
soothing those who cannot sleep
with its tireless, billowy call.

So as I lie awake worrying
about the emails I didn't send
at work today and how long
the project still has to run,
I'm lulled by wind that blew through war
and think of others lying here
through December 1944.

For hours they've been straining to hear
the chug... chug... of another doodlebug,
then the wait, a silent fall
preceding a whole terrace's demolition.
Waiting, still waiting,
but the only sound's the wind in the chimney,
that terrifying lullaby
we don't know whether to trust or shun.

2 – The Old Angel

Mutt scarf, pashmina pal, living stole,
he wore the dog across his shoulders.
One eye open, one eye closed, it dozed.
I think it's a cross-breed, he said with a wink.
A cross of a cross of a cross-breed.
He said he found it tied to a lamp-post,
and he freed it, and it followed him home.
Home? Home was everywhere and nowhere.
A fishmongers doorway. Among fruit stalls.
When he spoke his eyes shone like four cheap cans.
He breathed old Crombie, damp dog, Strongbow.
He claimed he'd mellowed. Gone were the days
he'd threaten to tear the arm off a man.
Come here, he said. Listen. The market's song.
Pound a bowl! Pound a bowl! What's wrong?

6

3 – A Perfect Circle

Leaving Epping, both bikes clean,
we ripped through the forest,
tore it from north to south
with two cuts of zipping tread.

Umber and lemon-ochre. Sunshine
filtered through beech and hornbeam.
Old friends not past trying
something new again.

We traded marriages and jobs
for mud-sputter and puddle-spit.
Got lost. Tonned it down hills
we couldn't see the bottom of.

Then we stopped. A clearing.
A solitary oak's first hard frost.
A perfect circle, flaming yellow,
laid down like the shock

of a summer dress slipped from
shoulders to pool on the floor.
We grinned like young lads
unused to sudden nakedness,

then pedalled on, keeping
a promise to be back before dark,
before the wind got up
and the leaves were squandered.

Hollyhocks

Yes, there were seven hollyhocks
in our garden, or was it six,
their tall stems covered in green knots
all through July, then gradually,

in early August, each bud burst
above us like summer fireworks,
an explosion of pinks and reds
that made us glad for hollyhocks,

and hopeful that immigrant seed
from the Ile de Ré would settle
in London, so we'd see again
English bees gorge on French pollen.

Sunflowers

Last week heads up, beaming, rapt,
carefree sun-worshippers with no hats,
a crowding of the credulous,
faithful followers of the one god,
happy shoppers queuing for the sales,
a stadium full of football fans, Tea Party
Americans, school pupils in assembly,
a whole regiment before their tour of duty,
festival goers, cinema goers, day-dream believers,
ballroom dancers before the dance,
optimists, the positive, company employees
on an annual away day,
awards ceremony attendees,
the loyal, the committed, deluded sycophants,
party members at an autumn conference.

This week downcast, dejected, defeated
semi-finalists, crestfallen, gutted,
workers informed of the factory closure,
community volunteers searching for a clue,
funeral attendees, members of the public
grieving for some star they never knew,
the lonely, the shamed, the guilty, sign-ups
for a pyramid scheme after the pyramid collapses,
the sorrowful, the lovelorn, any kind of victim,
gang members having their names taken,
fare dodgers, the collectively embarrassed,
the homeless, savers whose bank went bust
(but not the bankers),
populations scarred by life and death,
anyone who ever lived on this earth.

9

Euphrasy

Eyebright, unseen,
the euphrasy flowered all summer.

Its snapdragon lilac lobes
were cut down in a haze
or harvest blades around
mid-September and no-one
knows why

it lived through heat
and sunless days,
then the indifferent delays
of a farmhand waiting
for good weather.

Heading for the wood in June,
a young poet almost saw it
swaying beneath the corn-heads,
pause-ripening.

Undiscovered, undescribed, the swift
death of the euphrasy involved
no human loss or fault.

Camden Blooms

Hurrying up Delancey Street
my brow hooded to the rain,
breathing lungs-full of Columbia
past the coffee bean shop,
then mindful of nothing in particular
I hunch into Arlington Road
and notice the usual bunch of flowers
tied to a road sign are on the turn.

Give way the sign says,
the tips of their blood-red petals
just beginning to shrivel and brown—
and there's a message I've never read
about someone I couldn't have known.

But I wonder, being unfamiliar with grief,
if this is how it is, if this is how
the colour of loss gradually fades,
imperceptibly receding to a friable numbness.
Or whether it keeps renewing itself,
the devastation blooming afresh
like each new bunch of roses
tied tenderly to the road sign—
the shock of absence almost always there,
week after week, year after year.

Three Snooker Poems

1 – The Score

As his son, it was my job to keep score.
I'd squeeze onto the high-backed leather bench
in the dark corner away from the bar,
so it was easier to kneel and reach
the spot-lit mahogany board.
As each ball dropped I'd tot up
the points in my head, then
slide along his break in tens and units.

"Don't be addin' 'im any on lad,"
one of the men would say,
breaking out of a sullen, silent glare.
"Aye, but 'e could do wi' a few more,"
another would add, and they'd all
laugh and nod and cough as if
it was the funniest thing for months.
And they'd go quiet, lift glasses to mouths,
dip their lips in the froth.

Between breaks he'd stand next to me,
glancing over and over at the score,
chalking his cue more than he needed to.
I'd take nervous sips from my juice
and will the other man to miss.

Sometimes he'd ask me to pick the colours
from the pockets as well as keep score.
I'd walk round the table with all eyes on me,
waiting for me to slip up, stoop
to the hidden net for the cool, dark ball,

then reach into the limelight
to place it back on its spot.
God Bless You, I'd whisper to myself,
trying to remember where it should go.
God Green, Bless Brown, You Yellow.

2 – First Frame

The cue was a flag-pole
I pointed above.

The balls were distant planets
I'd forgotten the names of.

The table itself was a closely cropped field,
perfectly sunlit, endless, emerald.

I stood on the crate and he said here,
hold it like this, no, like this.

Your stance is the key
and your hand is a bridge,

lower your chin, bend one knee,
keep your head still,

don't close one eye, don't squint,
don't hit it too hard, don't... don't think.

Look at the white ball, then the red,
then the white, then the red.

Relax, it's a simple game.
What? No, really,

nice and easy, just push it through.
That's my boy, he said, you got one in.

I'm not playing you, beginner's luck.
Now then, you should clear up!

3 – The Con Club

We chased the fifteen reds
around a rectangle of light,
the curtained afternoon
rebuked a northern street.

I should have been at school,
but chose instead to learn
from chalking of the silence
between a father and his son.

The colours spurned the pockets,
the breaks were left unmade,
we supped our pints slowly,
stood the glasses side by side.

We never did the big talk
about the future or a girl,
but spent many quiet hours
in a darkened snooker hall.

Remembering Your Scent

Waking through a tangle of dreams,
instantly forgotten, I am born
into a brand new day.

I could be anyone, anywhere,
but put together in an instant
here and I and the sudden joy

of you, my love, by my side.
This is the familiar surprise:
together, we are still alive.

I lean over to kiss your cheek
and you murmur from the depths of sleep.
I inhale your skin, your hair,

trying to retain it, the scent,
but knowing that elsewhere,
next week, however much I try,

it will remain just out of reach.

Meeting Coleridge in St Michael's

Star-struck, muted, I'm sat next to Coleridge
on this old, oak pew. He's bigger than I'd
thought, quite a celebrity in the village,
though his lines are more referred to than read.
I should say something, introduce myself.
I want to tell him what it meant to me,
that second-hand book from the shortest shelf.
How it led me across other lands and sea,
to seek other versions down further roads.
How it dared me to dare to dream again,
to love all atmospheres, weathers and moods.
Saying nothing, I head out to the rain,
and being careful not to inflate his fame,
I tread softly on the worn flag of his tomb.

After Pieter de Hooch

He spent a lifetime
  trying to achieve
    the lay of light
      on a cloudy day
        on a tiled kitchen floor.

It meant something to him:
  a memory or a feeling
  or a memory of a feeling
  of being in an out of the way town
  on a cool, cloudy day.

Diluted light. Sunlight
  filtered through deep cloud
    that lies on terracotta tiles
      like the tired end of a long life.

Before he died he walked
  through the kitchen one last time
    and recognised the light, the tiles,
      the open doorway of a provincial house
        to be a fair facsimile of his own art.

Morandi

I

Only a small green bottle
placed by a dusty window
on a slow sunless afternoon.

Only the light dallying through
glass as though uninterested
in the world's finer detail.

II

The pleasure he took from laying it on thick:
pale blocks of ochre, umber, cool terracotta,
his life pared down to a studio-cum-bedroom,
a table of vases, jugs, unlabelled bottles,
a few jars of brushes, paint, clean canvasses,
a mean light and shadow from an only window.

Meditation On Mundane

After buying a postcard of Edward Hopper's 'Automat'

As with Vermeer, I love the way Hopper observes
the subtle shadows in the corners of rooms.
Down by the radiator for example, the way the light
would slant through the door like that whatever her mood,
but in their listless unswept stillness the shadows
seem to contribute to the heaviness of her thoughts,
are helpless beside the window of the large black night
and her sudden aloneness passing through it.

Cold as a window-pane to the touch, her gloveless fingers
curl loosely around the bathroom blue coffee cup
and are indifferent to the carefully coloured details
of Hopper's vision: the bowl of red fruit,
the fluorescent light bounded by glass,
the raw sienna radiator and its loveless shadow.

Whom she left and all the months of worry
have been distilled into this momentary stare,
locked into this infinite miserable night
for which this woman will always be remembered.
Picture the unthinkable anguish of not knowing
whether you've done the right thing,
the painstakingly unseen shadows down by the radiator,
the great molared jaws of night.

The Gardener

Hunched over, he fed the stove with touchwood:
browned wings of pine and fern, then scraps of paper
to get it going. The evening distilled
to a crackle of dry twigs, nurtured fire
and the present memory of wood-smoke.

Surrounded by cold-frames, flower-pots, broken
trellises, the gardener lived in an old shack
in the dark heart of the wood. A weather-worn,
involuntary hermit, he welcomed visitors
like the first snowdrops of spring. The pot boiled
so he poured me tea in a small, chipped vase.

Then, in clotting twilight we sat and listened
to the loud silence of cicadas, content
to be there and have no more to talk about.

The Small Wild Goose Pagoda At Xian

Stones rising from an eighth century winter
embody a clear memory of cold: tower of time.
Branch shadows are at their best in November,
gentle and consequential as palm lines,
but the pale, polluted sun tenders only an inner warmth:
that bare sepulchral glow felt on late afternoons
by tired builders who attested to the tiered growth of rock,
the slow displacement of sky.

We scale it, as we have done every year,
then walk around the back to find the old bronze bell.
Out of place, brought down by lightning,
its stubborn cast of characters, unreadable now,
speak of the simple roots of language.
I rap my knuckles on its armoured side
and listen to the courtyard's lasting peace
snuff out remembrance of that first chime.

The Procession

Watching the procession
of the water buffalo
the plough and the man

it is hard to imagine
he is holding the train
of her ivory dress

and her slow-stepping
muddled stride is approaching
a version of grace.

Slap

A bowl of water thrown
from an open door-way

still surprises me less
than the gradual flat slap

soaking the dust-blown road.

The Lemon Ant Tree

A hundred metres into the rainforest, Diego held his hand up.
We stopped, gathered round in our wellies and sweat
to look at the twig he'd broken off.

He sliced it lengthways with the edge of his knife
and the ants tumbled out of their symbiotic life
like people from a theatre at the end of the play,
rushing in all directions across the broad piazza of his hand.

"Go on, try some," he said.
He was looking at me, and though I'd been vegetarian
for the best part of a decade, it seemed rude to refuse.
I popped a few of them onto my tongue, swallowed,
then had to agree with Diego that they did indeed taste of
    lemon.
Even so, I couldn't help but imagine them running around
    inside me,
up and down the trunks of my legs, along the branches of
    my arms,
the twigs of my fingers.

Walking With My Father

Reverting to this hill
in a further lifetime,
I will follow the walk
we took today
after the rain cleared
and blaze of November
sunshine roused
the sodden land.

Muted in loss,
I will follow the two
of us across limestone
and blue moor-grass,
noting that distinctive
roll of your shoulders,
our thinning hair,
listening in as our talk
dips and climbs through
the few prevailing trails
of our disparate lives.

Then stopping,
as we both stopped,
I will linger in our
abiding silence
to breathe in
the far, forfeited view
across Wharfedale.

And later, much later,
I will see this day
as a tall blade of grass
blowing gently apart
from the others,
or sundown warming
the greening staff
of an old, opened,
wooden gate.

Father's Day

Interrupting another of his unfinished watercolours,
my call must be like many on this day for fathers.
As usual, we ask after each other and our wives,
filling in the opaque interstices of our distant lives.

Then he tells me, while laying on another moor-green wash,
that just this morning they finished baling the back field.
"The stubble is all gold," he says, and I feel the loss
of the view from my old bedroom and the hours it filled.

On mid-summer evenings when bed-time was too early
   for sleep:
parted curtains, reek of hay, the cool sill and hypnotic drop
of bale after bale. "Dad," I say. "Dad, are you still there?"
Silence, then the swish of his best sable brush in the jam-jar.